Sorted
in 30 days
MONEY

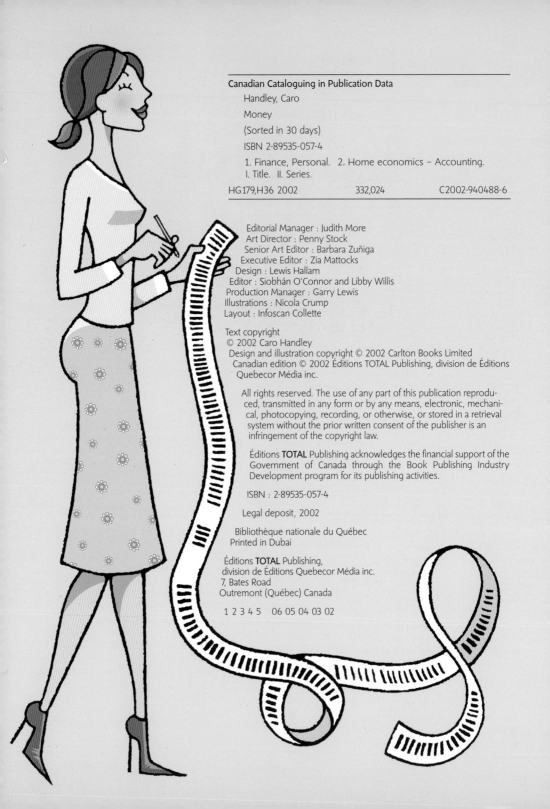

Canadian Cataloguing in Publication Data

Handley, Caro

Money

(Sorted in 30 days)

ISBN 2-89535-057-4

1. Finance, Personal. 2. Home economics – Accounting.
I. Title. II. Series.

HG179.H36 2002   332,024   C2002-940488-6

Editorial Manager : Judith More
Art Director : Penny Stock
Senior Art Editor : Barbara Zuñiga
Executive Editor : Zia Mattocks
Design : Lewis Hallam
Editor : Siobhán O'Connor and Libby Willis
Production Manager : Garry Lewis
Illustrations : Nicola Crump
Layout : Infoscan Collette

Text copyright
© 2002 Caro Handley
Design and illustration copyright © 2002 Carlton Books Limited
Canadian edition © 2002 Éditions TOTAL Publishing, division de Éditions
Quebecor Média inc.

Éditions **TOTAL** Publishing acknowledges the financial support of the
Government of Canada through the Book Publishing Industry
Development program for its publishing activities.

ISBN : 2-89535-057-4

Legal deposit, 2002

Bibliothèque nationale du Québec
Printed in Dubai

Éditions **TOTAL** Publishing,
division de Éditions Quebecor Média inc.
7, Bates Road
Outremont (Québec) Canada

1 2 3 4 5   06 05 04 03 02

Sorted
in 30 days
MONEY

how to organize your finances
in just one month

caro handley

ÉDITIONS TOTAL PUBLISHING

Contents

Introduction   7

Day 1: Money matters   8   Day 17: About that rainy day   46

Day 2: Your beliefs   11   Day 18: Attracting more   48

Day 3: Self-esteem   13   Day 19: Be your own best adviser 50

Day 4: Where has it all gone?   16   Day 20: Stay independent   52

Day 5: Stop being an ostrich   18   Day 21: Make good choices   55

Day 6: Take control   21   Day 22: Money for fun   57

Day 7: What you want   23   Day 23: Going wild   60

Day 8: Keep it simple   26   Day 24: Comfort spending   62

Day 9: What goes out   28   Day 25: Give it away   65

Day 10: What comes in   30   Day 26: Look after the small change 67

Day 11: Be honest   32   Day 27: Money and moods   70

Day 12: The cost of your job   35   Day 28: Trust   72

Day 13: Cancel the crises   37   Day 29: Set your aims   74

Day 14: Shared finances   40   Day 30: Celebrate!   76

Day 15: Money mistakes   42   A Final Word   78

Day 16: Dealing with debt   44   Resources   80

Introduction

We *all* deserve financial security, abundance and the skills and confidence to manage money in our lives. You deserve these things – and you can have them. Not one day in the future, but right now. No matter how dire your financial situation, you can turn it around and feel confident and successful with money if you really want to. Learn how to enjoy money instead of worrying about it. To avoid debt and be in control. To feel rich instead of poor.

Of course, it takes time to learn new money habits and make them part of your life. You can, however, put the stepping stones in place very easily. Once you are feeling differently about money, once you are in control and know how to handle and manage money, it will far easier to make your new habits second nature.

There is so much money in the world – enough for all of us to meet our needs and have plenty left for saving and spending. To attract the money you want into your life, you need to know how to manage money, how to be generous with it, how to keep it flowing and how to treat it with respect but never fear. In this book, I will show you how, in 30 days, your attitude to money and the role of money in your life can be transformed. Follow the steps and choose to be successful with money and to live a life of financial ease.

Day One

MONEY MATTERS

Today I want you to look at the role of money in your life. Like it or not, money is important. Everyone needs it and needs to know how to use it, manage it and bring it into their lives. Some people seem naturally brilliant with money, attracting loads of it and surrounding themselves with luxury. Others are simply comfortable with it and never worry. Then there are those who never seem to have enough, worry a lot and spend what little they do have too fast, or hang on to it so tightly that they can never enjoy what they have.

What's your relationship with money?

See which of the following descriptions sounds like you. Tick all those that ring true, then add any more that occur to you. You may identify with more than one:

- You earn plenty of money, but spend it even faster than you earn it.
- You make a reasonable amount and muddle through, but don't really feel on top of things financially.
- You sit tight on your money and agonize about every expense.
- You can handle the day-to-day stuff, but the bigger things such as pensions and investments are a mystery.
- You don't have any idea how to organize your money. You feel out of control when it comes to your finances.
- You're always broke and, when you feel down, spend money you don't have.
- You have a very low income and you're sick of struggling.
- You're always borrowing from friends or family, taking out loans or running up overdrafts.
- You have no idea how much you actually owe, but it's probably a lot.
- You feel ashamed of the mess you make with money and yet you're reluctant to seek help.

However many of these statements are true of you, don't feel like a failure. You're not alone! The majority of people have trouble handling money, overspend, feel that they don't have enough and worry. A great number of people overspend. And, for many people, having money troubles leads to low self-esteem and anxiety.

The good news is that these are problems that can be solved. Absolutely anyone can learn to be good with money. There's no mystery, miracle or hard-to-learn skill about it. All you need is resolve, staying power and the willingness to do things differently and pull your head out of the sand. Decide today that you're going to make money your friend, rather than your enemy. Choose financial success, rather than failure.

You can choose to be good with money right now

Day Two

YOUR BELIEFS

Now I want you to examine your beliefs about money. One key thing in life that can hold us back more than anything else is our belief system. Why? Because our thoughts are based on our beliefs, and our actions are a result of our thoughts. In other words, everything we think and do stems from our beliefs. Here's an example.

Claudia believed that she didn't deserve to have a lot of money. She also believed that she would never earn more than her older sister, who had done better at school and had been considered the 'clever' one in the family. As a result, Claudia took a boring job and told herself she must put up with it. She was so convinced of this that, when she was offered promotion, she turned it down. She was afraid that she wouldn't cope. Then she was offered a better job elsewhere, which she also turned down.

Claudia was determined to prove her beliefs true. It was only after she decided to change her beliefs that she took action. She found a better job, earned more and soon realized she was excellent at what she did. Within three years, she was a star in the company and was earning more than her sister.

What were Claudia's new beliefs? That she could do anything she wanted and that she was talented and deserved to be well rewarded and earn a great salary.

Root out the beliefs that hold you back

Do you identify with any of these? Tick the ones that apply and add more of your own:

- I'm hopeless with money.
- I'll never earn much.
- Other people have plenty of money, not me.
- Money just slips through my fingers.
- I don't deserve to have money.
- Money is dirty – you can't be rich and be a good person.
- I'll never be in control of my money.
- Bills and demands are scary – I dread them.
- There isn't enough money to go round.
- I'm always afraid that my money will run out.

All these beliefs stem from a poverty mentality. The majority of people think in this 'there will never be enough' way.

Now choose to let those beliefs go and to adopt some new ones. It's time to shift into abundance mentality and to welcome money into your life.

Use any of the following beliefs, plus some of your own:

- There's more than enough to go round.
- You can have lots of money and be a good person.
- I deserve to have a life filled with abundance.
- I can earn all the money I want.
- I respect all my bills, grateful for whatever I am paying for and knowing I can pay them easily.
- I manage my money well, knowing I can be generous and still have plenty left.
- I find it easy to control my money.
- I'm great with money.
- I choose to enjoy my money, knowing there will always be enough.

Once you have chosen your new beliefs, repeat them to yourself often and say them out loud when you can. Whenever an old, unhelpful belief pops up in your mind, just replace it instantly with a new belief. Remember that our beliefs are simply a measure of the way we see the world. We can choose our attitude and our beliefs, and by doing so encourage our life to follow the path we have chosen.

Choose to believe in abundance and feel instantly richer

Day Three

SELF-ESTEEM

Today is the day for examining your self-esteem in relation to money. Self-esteem can vary in different areas of our lives. You may feel confident in and proud of your work, but self-doubting and uncertain in relationships.

How are you when it comes to money? The level of your monetary self-esteem will have a huge impact on your financial success and the way in which you deal with money matters. Put simply, self-esteem is the way you feel about yourself.

To find out what your self-esteem is really like around money, answer the following:

- Do you often worry about money?
- Do you doubt your ability to earn the amount you'd like?
- Do you often find yourself in debt?
- Does your heart sink when you think about money?
- Do you feel guilty when you do have money?
- Do you find yourself spending it as fast as you get it?
- Do you hide the amount of money you have?

If you answered yes to any of these questions, your self-esteem in regard to money matters is not as high as it could be. If you answered yes to three or more, your self-esteem is definitely low.

When you have low self-esteem in relation to money, it stops you bringing money into your life, being able to enjoy it or being able to hold on to it. Either you can't earn the amount you'd like or you earn well but spend it as fast as you can so that you won't have the pleasure of having it. Or perhaps you have money, but refuse to enjoy it and treat yourself. Whatever the case, now is the time to make changes.

Here is a simple guide to raising your self-esteem:

- Treat yourself in the way that you would a good friend: with kindness and compassion, understanding and forgiveness.
- Focus on your strengths, rather than what you consider to be your faults and weaknesses.
- Nurture yourself, and help yourself to grow.
- Talk to yourself in positive ways, appreciating all your achievements.
- Cultivate self-belief by encouraging and praising yourself.
- If you are weighed down by painful, unresolved issues from your past, be willing to let them go and move on. Try to forgive everyone, including yourself. Remember that every day you have the choice between happiness and unhappiness, and that past hurts can be a source of great strength in the present.

Raising your self-esteem will benefit all areas of your life, not just your finances. Feeling good about yourself will lead to feeling in control, making better judgements and drawing more money into your life. You will also be able to stop spending money recklessly simply to cheer yourself up or comfort yourself.

Raise your self-esteem in relation to money and feel empowered

Day Four

WHERE HAS IT ALL GONE?

Today it's crunch time – time to think
about where all the money you've had
in your life so far has gone and whether
you're happy with the choices you have
made. We live in a society in which
material things are very important. Most of us
have a wishlist of things we'd like to own. Most of us already own a great deal. We
also live in a society where spending is encouraged, whether or not we have money.
We spend on goods, holidays, entertainment and gambling – to name just a few.
Look around you. The things in your home are money turned into goods. Almost
everything you have cost money. How much money is there in the room with you?

We choose the way we spend our money. Understanding the choices you have
made and deciding whether you are happy with those choices are vital first steps
to making changes.

Exercise

Take a pen and piece of paper, and write a list
of things you have spent money on in the past
three years. You might include:

- Training courses or classes.
- Material goods, such as CD players,
  computers, electrical goods or kitchen
  equipment, for example.
- Mortgage or rent.
- Bills.
- Clothes and shoes, make-up, accessories.
- Travel.
- Entertainment – meals out, films, shows, clubs.
- Loans and debt repayment.
- Alcohol or drugs.

Be totally honest when making your list. Then highlight the three areas where you spend the most. Think about how important these are to you and how you feel about your spending in these areas. Answer the following questions:

- Are you happy with the amount you have spent in each of these three categories?
- Are you happy with what you have to show for your spending? Are the things you paid for important, useful or a source of pleasure for you?
- Are these three categories the most important to you and the right priorities?
- What changes would you make now if you could?

The answers to these questions will give you key information about your spending patterns and the way you feel about them. You should, by now, have a clearer idea of some of the changes you want and need to make. If you've been overspending on unnecessary things, or avoiding important areas, it's time to use your money in different ways.

Investigating how you spend your money is a concrete step towards making changes

Day Five

STOP BEING AN OSTRICH

This is when I want you to pull your head out of the sand and stop being an ostrich. How do I know that's what you're doing? Well, anyone who is not comfortable, clear about and happy with the way she or he handles money is being an ostrich about money in some way.

Being an ostrich means being in denial – in other words, hiding, pretending or ignoring a truth about the way you spend your money. As long as you do this, you will never feel in control of money or really good about the money you have. It's the same as tying a blindfold around your head, then wondering why you're always in the dark when it comes to your financial situation.

What are the ways in which you're being an ostrich? Be honest with yourself. Are you doing any of the following?:

- Ignoring bank statements or bills.
- Running up credit-card debts.
- Keeping a permanent and dangerously swelling overdraft.
- Depending too much on something you can't afford at the cost of areas where you should be putting your money.
- Trying to keep up with people who have more money than you.
- Trusting that everything will somehow work out in the end.
- Getting caught in the grip of a spending obsession – shoes, bags, clothes.
- Comfort spending to avoid painful feelings.
- Attempting to buy love.
- Pretending to be someone you're not in order to impress.
- Gambling excessively in any way.
- Submitting to blackmail.
- Supporting another adult who is capable of supporting himself or herself.
- Investing in something suspect or uncertain.
- Promising yourself a fresh start with money – over and over again.

If you're doing any one of these things – or several of them – you're being an ostrich. Time to stop! Why? Because being an ostrich is:

- Uncomfortable.
- Difficult and stressful to keep up.
- A waste of energy and time.
- A way to keep yourself poor.
- A manner of inviting things to get worse.
- Always unrewarding and often damaging.

When you decide to stop being an ostrich, you'll feel a surge of relief and you'll be taking a big step towards financial freedom and abundance. All you have to do right now is to become absolutely clear about where and how you're being an ostrich. Once you've recognized what you're doing, you can choose to stop. Have you had enough of burying your head in the sand, of the uncomfortable feelings that go with it and of living in a financial fog? Great! Then make the decision to stop. Today.

Leave being an ostrich in the past and know your worth

Day Six

TAKE CONTROL

Today I want you to make the decision to take control of your money and the way you use it. Most people, if asked to think about it, feel that money is controlling them and not the other way around. Even the phrases people use give this attitude away. Do you ever use, or hear, the following?:

- I wish I could, but I haven't got enough money.
- If only we had the money.
- I hate money.
- I never have the money for what I really want.
- Money's such a bore.
- Money just disappears.
- I don't know what happens to it all.
- I dread bills – they just eat my money.
- The cost of things these days is horrific – I can't afford the things I want.

It's as though the money chose to disappear, or chose the way it was being spent, rather than you managing it. Make an effort today to watch the way you talk about money and to stop using phrases that make you sound weak and powerless in relation to it. Instead, begin to think of yourself as strong and successful with money. Recognize that the way you spend your money is your choice.

- Instead of saying: 'I can't afford it,' say: 'I'd rather save my money for other things.'
- Instead of 'I hate money,' say: 'I love money, it brings all kinds of good things into my life and I enjoy managing it well.'
- Instead of 'Money just disappears,' say: 'I always know how much money I have and what I'm choosing to spend it on.'
- Instead of 'I dread bills,' say: 'I pay my bills with pleasure, knowing I can afford them and appreciating the benefits and services they bring.'
- Instead of 'The cost of things is horrific,' say: 'I always choose to spend my money on things which are good value and worthwhile.'

Changing the way you talk and think about money will revolutionize your attitude towards money and bring more of it into your life. Begin to think, talk and behave as though you are in clear and firm control of your money, and refuse ever to think of things the other way around. Instead of letting money be an overlord, a burden or a source of worry, choose to make it an ally, a source of freedom and a pleasure.

Choose to say no to resentment, frustration and lack. Say yes to control, to calm and free choice, and to plenty.

**Be in control of your money and
know that the choice is yours**

Day Seven

WHAT YOU WANT

This is the day you're going to have fun making your financial wishlist. Before you start listing all the things you'd love to buy and have and do, however, I want you to think very carefully. Don't rush straight to the designer stilettos, the skiing holiday and the expensive top-to-toe beauty treatments.

On this wishlist, I want you to put the things which would really bring you peace of mind, a sense of security and joy. They may not be the things you think of first. Sometimes, the biggest benefits come from spending your money on things which seem boring and worthy. It may surprise you, when you think long and hard about it, to find out what you really want.

Here are some ideas for your wishlist:

- Buying your own home.
- Paying off your mortgage if you already have one.
- Accumulating savings.
- Joining a pension fund (the younger you start, the cheaper they are!).
- Learning about wise investments.
- Having enough ready for Christmas so that you don't end up flat-broke in January.

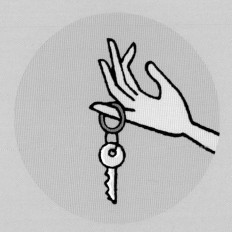

- Knowing that you have enough and are comfortable.
- Never borrowing money again.
- Never fearing bank managers/landlords/credit-card companies again.

It's easy to wish for sudden wealth and to imagine that this would end all your problems. The reality is, however, that most people are very unsettled by sudden wealth. It takes them out of their comfort zone and catapults them into a whole new set of challenges and problems.

It's better by far to be wise enough to know what would work well for you and what is sufficient. How much would you need in order to feel comfortable and happy? To stop worrying? It's probably far less than you imagined at first, as the real art of comfort and freedom from worry is good management and abundance consciousness.

By all means include fun things and luxuries on your wishlist. In fact, they're very important – everyone needs them. But before you get to them, work out the basics, the things you need to put in place to feel great about your money and your life. Once you've identified these, think about a timescale for making them happen. Add this to your list, beside each item. So it might read: 'Own my own home within three years, pay off debts within six months, start saving now.'

Know that everything on your wishlist is possible, and that it's up to you to make it happen. Think about the steps you'll need to take to begin doing this. Feel the joy and pleasure of knowing that it's up to you and that you can grant your own wishes.

Wish for what you want and make it come true

Day Eight

KEEP IT SIMPLE

It's time now to begin managing your money in ways that you can sustain for the rest of your life. The wonderful thing about managing money is that, once you've got the hang of it, you never forget it again – just like riding a bicycle or salsa dancing!

The best truth of all is that managing money is simple and should always be kept simple. If anyone tries to make it complicated or tells you it's complicated, don't believe them. It isn't, and it need never be.

To manage your money well, you need to observe some basic rules:

- You must know what you spend.
- You must know what your income is.
- Your spending must be less than your income.
- You must keep an accurate, up-to-date record of all your income and spending.

And that's about it.

What you don't need are endless accounts books, 15 bank accounts, complex computer spreadsheets and daily study of the financial newspapers. Here's what you need to organize your money in a simple and effective way:

- A current or working account with a bank, building society or credit union.
- All your regular bills paid automatically from your current or working account.
- A savings account.
- A regular payment from your current or working account into your savings account, so that your savings grow almost without you noticing.
- One credit card which you use for emergencies only – or at the very least judiciously – and the bill for which you repay in full each month.
- A ruled exercise book for record keeping.
- A file for bank statements and other financial documents.
- A couple of hours once a month to check your bank statements against your records and to pay any outstanding or one-off bills.

These can all be organized if you put your mind to it. So set the wheels in motion – today. Once your money management has been simplified, your whole life becomes simpler. You'll free up time and energy for other things, and money worries will diminish.

Here's how to keep your record book:

1 Divide the page into four columns.
2 At the top of the first column, write 'DATE'.
3 At the top of the second, write 'IN'.
4 At the top of the third, write 'OUT'.
5 At the top of the fourth, write 'BALANCE'.

Keep this record daily. It takes only a minute or two to add any transactions you've made that day, and this way you will always know what the balance of your current or working account should be.

Remember that it's always best to know what you have – and what you don't. That way, you can make decisions about what needs changing and about what you spend. Avoiding knowing simply causes problems. To know what you're dealing with is to choose solutions over worry and wisdom over ignorance.

Keep it simple and choose to be a winner with money

Day Nine

WHAT GOES OUT

This is the day to take the next step in managing your money well. In order to put the first of the basic rules in place, you must know exactly what you spend. If you haven't organized and managed your money before, this will probably be a grey area. It may be a bit blurry round the edges or it may be a complete fog! Whichever it is, don't worry. Just make the decision to dispel the mists and to come clean with yourself about what you spend your money on.

Where does your money go?

Take a pen and piece of paper, and write down the categories you need to include. These are:

- Rent or mortgage.
- Bills – gas, electricity, telephone.
- Insurance – house, car.
- Club memberships.
- Credit-card bills.
- Store-card repayments, rental agreements.
- Food.
- Clothes and accessories.
- Cosmetics and toiletries.
- Entertainment and leisure.
- Travel (not including holidays).
- Petrol and car expenses, if you have one.

Add any other categories that apply to you. Now begin to fill them in. You need to know what you spend on a monthly basis. Use any documents you have that will help, such as bank statements, bills or receipts. Where you don't know the amount, put an estimate. When you've finished, you'll have an idea of what you spend. It's unlikely to be completely accurate, but it will give you something to work from.

Over the next month, write down in a notebook every single amount you spend, however small. Carry the book around with you and get into the habit of noting any money you spend as soon as you spend it. You won't need to keep doing this for ever (unless you want to), but it's important to do it for at least a month, or even two or three, so that you know exactly what you are spending. You may find that some of your estimates were way out. You may be surprised by how much you spend on food, cosmetics or petrol.

If you live with a partner or friends, you must work out your share of the expenses. It's vital that things are fairly divided and that you agree on this. You can then take care of your share and let the other person or people deal with their side of things.

Writing down all your spending is an eye-opening exercise and one that is well worth doing. You'll never again be able to say: 'I don't know where it goes!' You'll open the door to choices and flexibility in the way you use your money.

Know what goes out and you have the key to change

Day Ten

WHAT COMES IN

So, you have dealt with how your money goes out. Now you need to look at the money that comes in – in other words, your income, from whatever source. In order to manage your money in a simple and satisfying way, this half of the equation has to be filled in.

Yesterday's exercise may have been tough. You may have been amazed by the amount you spend. Today should be more fun, even if you think your income is too low. As you do today's exercise, think abundance. Feel rich at the thought of the money that comes to you. Recognize how lucky you are and that this money is yours, to use as you choose.

Where does your money come from?

Take a pen and piece of paper, and write down all the regular elements of your income, no matter how small the amount. Make sure you include (if applicable):

- Earnings from your job/s.
- Grants.
- Interest on savings.
- Dividends.
- Rent paid to you.
- State benefits.
- Maintenance for yourself or your children.

Add any other categories that apply to you. Now fill in all the categories, using wage slips; bank, building society or post office records; and any other relevant documents you have. At the end, add everything up to come up with a monthly income total.

Now you need to compare this figure with the monthly expenditure figure that you worked out yesterday. To achieve financial peace of mind, it's essential for the income figure to be higher than the expenditure figure.

If your income figure is higher than your expenditure figure, that's fine. You have a good basis from which to work. You can think about using any excess for saving, paying off any debts and loans, or having a 'fun' fund. If the two figures are about even, that's okay, too, as long as you're happy with the way you're spending your money and don't mind not having a safety net. If the expenditure figure is higher than the income figure, you need to make changes.

Don't panic and start planning to move, live on baked beans or pull out the telephone socket. Do, however, think about what would be needed to bring your figures into line. Perhaps you could earn more? Perhaps you could make fairly simple adjustments, such as buying fewer clothes? Perhaps you need to make bigger changes, such as moving somewhere cheaper or selling your car. It's your decision, and it's you who will feel the benefits.

Know what is coming in and appreciate these riches

Day Eleven

BE HONEST

Today it's time to look at whether you're totally honest with yourself – and other people – about what you do with your money. Don't be alarmed by the idea that you might be less than truthful. Almost everyone is, often without even realizing it. It takes courage and integrity to venture into every dusty little corner of your finances and to be absolutely honest with yourself. But it's worth doing, as it will bring you peace of mind and freedom from worry.

Think about what might be going on that's less than completely honest. If you've got debts, that's a clue, as we often kid ourselves and fib to ourselves to justify debt. Here are some ways in which we're not always upfront about money. See whether any of these apply to you:

- You keep money secrets from the people to whom you're closest.
- You make excuses to yourself to justify credit-card debts or loans.
- You accept money gifts (for instance, hand-outs from your parents), even when they make you feel uncomfortable and childlike.
- You count the same bit of income three times when making spending decisions.
- You never look at bank statements and bills.
- You put things on credit cards when you know you can't afford them.
- You know you need to make changes, but you keep putting them off.
- You fiddle your tax.
- You tell lies about money to another person – anyone at all.
- You rely on your partner for an income when there's no good reason why you shouldn't earn your own.

There are many other ways in which we can be less than totally honest about money. None of them feels good. Being dishonest, even in small ways, leaves you feeling bad about yourself. Even if no one else knows you're cheating, YOU KNOW!

Make the decision today to be completely honest. Begin with yourself. Root out all the secrets, tricks and cons, and junk them. Decide what you're going to do differently, and take action. Then tell anyone else who needs to know.

For instance, if you've decided to stand on your own two feet and stop taking money from parents or a partner, sort out what the alternatives are, then tell the person or people concerned in a warm and mature way. Don't forget to thank them for their generosity and support, even if you suspect that they may have used money to control you. Remember that it was your choice to accept it.

Or, if you never bother to check bank statements and bills, make a resolution to do so from now on. Schedule a regular time each month, and mark every one in your diary for the year. When it comes time to do it, look on it not as a chore, but as a challenge – a project you want to complete to the best of your ability and from which you can only gain. When you've finished, reward yourself with a treat. And, you never know, you may spot a mistake that means the bank owes you money!

Be honest, be clear and set yourself free

Day Twelve

THE COST OF YOUR JOB

It's time to look at the true cost of your job. This may sound strange at first, but it's important to understand that we all pay a price for the jobs we do and to be sure that you consider the price of yours worth paying.

What do I mean by the price we pay? Here are some examples:

- Working long hours.
- Being undermined or put down by someone.
- Becoming a monster who orders everyone around.
- Having to stay silent when you know what the answer is.

- Doing something too easy for you and feeling frustrated.
- Feeling like a dogsbody.
- Taking part in something harmful or unethical.
- Having to make all the decisions and feeling alone and unsupported.
- Being a part of something which doesn't fit with your beliefs or the kind of person you are.
- Doing something which damages your personal life.

There are many other potential downsides to any job. It's very important that you recognize any that affect you and weigh them against the good aspects of your work. Of course, the good aspects may far outweigh the price you are paying. If so, that's fine. But be true to yourself. Never hang on in a job through fear that you won't find another one or won't succeed elsewhere. There is always another possibility, always an alternative, always the potential for a fresh start.

People who love their work tend to be the ones who succeed financially, too. Doing something you love will motivate you to give your best, and it may bring you rewards such as promotion, bonuses or a pay rise. But there are also people who hang on in jobs they hate because the money is good. If you are one of them, think again. Money alone is never a good enough reason to compromise your wellbeing. If you work for money alone, you'll never truly enjoy the job and feel good about it. Feel proud of the way you earn your living and you'll be able to enjoy your money and attract more of it to you.

Spend today weighing up the price you are paying for your job. If you feel, deep down, that it's time to make a change, begin to look around for a job which is truly right for you. Expect to be fairly rewarded, but don't be driven by money. If you take care of yourself by finding the right kind of job for you, the financial side will take care of itself. Be brave, be bold and be proud of what you do.

**If the price you pay for your job is too high,
find the courage to let it go**

Day Thirteen

CANCEL THE CRISES

Today will be devoted to money crises and what can be done about them. Are you one of those people who has regular money crises? Is your financial life a constant rollercoaster of highs and lows that create all sorts of problems? Are you often in the middle of some kind of financial drama or upset? If so, it's time to look at different ways of doing things.

Here are some examples of financial crises. See whether any of them apply to you:

- A huge bill has arrived, and you can't pay it.
- Someone you borrowed money from wants it back right now.
- The money from the remortgage/loan you took out has all gone and you need to borrow more.
- The credit-card company is threatening to take you to court.
- The mortgage/rent is in arrears.
- The cheque you're expecting hasn't arrived and your bank account is empty.
- You've gone over your overdraft limit yet again, and you're being stung for massive interest charges.
- The hot-water system has blown up and you can't afford a new one.

- Payday is two weeks away and you're broke.
- The gas/electricity/telephone has been cut off because you didn't pay the bill, but you don't even remember receiving it.
- You've had to grovel to the bank manager/your parents/your landlord yet again, and you're getting sick of their patronizing expressions.

Does any of this seem familiar? People who go in for financial crises tend to have them regularly and to experience a variety. They're tedious, scary, exhausting – and exasperating for everyone else. So why does anyone do it? It's partly lack of good money management, but there's another part to it. Every financial crisis has its pay-off – in other words, its reward. Often this is the relief when the crisis has been sorted out. People who lurch from one crisis to another are often addicted to the feelings of anxiety followed by relief. But the good news is ...

You need never have another financial crisis again!

It's that simple. Make the decision today to reorganize your finances, to live within your means and to put money aside for emergencies. Free yourself from the burden of financial crises. Get off the high–low rollercoaster, and give yourself the gift of peace of mind. Use the skill with which you sort out crises to avoid them in the first place.

Financial crises drain you – let them go and feel the freedom

Day Fourteen

SHARED FINANCES

Today is for focusing on the question of shared finances. It may be that you already share some financial responsibilities with another person. Perhaps you have a flatmate or a partner. If you don't, you can be sure that you will, at some point, need to make joint financial decisions with another person and to share your finances with them.

Between friends and flatmates, these issues should be easily sorted out, as your money stays separate. You simply decide who is responsible for what. If complications arise, you can deal with them or move on. Between partners, however, financial issues are more complex and can become a source of conflict. So, it's just as well to get the rules really clear from the start, so that you're prepared for the best way to manage things and need never let money come between you.

Everyone has a different attitude towards money and different ideas about what's important. Finding a way to agree on the basics and live with the differences is one of life's most valuable skills.

Managing joint finances

1 Always keep your independence. Have a joint account for joint responsibilities, but keep your own account, too, containing some money which is yours to spend as you wish.

2 Never hand over the management of finances to the other person. It's fine for one of you to do the day-to-day accounting, but the other one should know what's going on and join in all decisions. If you leave everything to your partner, you put yourself in a childlike position; if you're the one who does it all, you may end up feeling burdened and over-controlling. Either way, you'll both be resentful.

3 Decide which areas of expenditure are joint, and either allocate them between you or both pay money into a joint account to cover them.

4 Be honest with each other about what matters to you. If you want to save but your partner wants to spend, work out a compromise and stick to it. Always listen to the other person's point of view, and be willing to negotiate. Let go of the idea that one of you is right and the other is wrong.

5 If you stop work – for instance, to have children – make sure that you still have spending money of your own. You're still contributing to the family, and you shouldn't have to ask your partner for every little bit of money you need.

6 Plan for a future that isn't completely dependent on staying together. Divorced women often end up poor because they relied too much on their husband's earnings. Have your own assets and money that will be yours no matter what.

Organizing your finances jointly is a challenge for most couples, especially if you've managed your money on your own for a long time. Do it gently, with humour and understanding. Even if you come up against a frustrating and difficult situation, remember that miracles can be worked with tenderness and love, whereas anger and criticism will only create blocks.

Learning to manage money with another person can be exciting, fun and rewarding

Day Fifteen

MONEY MISTAKES

Okay, this is the point where you have to face up to money mistakes. Why? Because every single one of us has made them and will make more of them. No one manages money perfectly, and most people get quite a lot of things wrong.

Perhaps you've even made the same mistake twice – or several times. If this is the case, there's something important to be learnt from this type of mistake, and, when you learn it, you will no longer need to keep making it. Life often gives us the same lesson over and over again until we learn what we need to know.

So, if you're feeling bad about any mistakes you may have made, large or small, relax. Mistakes are simply there to show us the way forward and to teach us how to manage better in the future. Learn from them, and they become gifts.

Here are some of the mistakes that people commonly make. Do any of them strike a chord with you?:

- Splashing out on something which turns out to be a dud, such as a timeshare holiday apartment you hardly, if ever, use or an expensive outfit you never actually wear.
- Spending more than you earn and having to borrow to make up the difference.
- Investing in something which goes bust or loses value badly.
- Thinking that spending money will magically make you feel better if you're feeling low or broken-hearted.
- Taking on financial responsibilities that you think you can cope with, then finding that they're just too expensive and you're constantly worrying.
- Lending money that you never get back.

If you've made any of these mistakes, or any others that aren't listed, you should take comfort from that fact that you're not alone. These mistakes are all very common. The good news is that you need never make them again.

Avoiding money mistakes
- Think very carefully before you spend any large sum of money. It's easy to be drawn into the excitement of a timeshare (the sales people are experts) or a new outfit, or anything else. But it will generally always be there the next day (despite what they say!), so consider it overnight, check it out thoroughly if necessary and only go ahead if you're sure.
- Impulse buy with only very small amounts of money.
- If you want to go out and spend to cheer yourself up, decide how much you can afford to blow and only take that amount with you in cash.
- When you take on the responsibilities of a mortgage, work out what you think you could afford, then reduce it by a third. It's better to have money to spare than to be trapped with costs you can't manage.
- Never lend money that you can't afford to lose. Either treat the loan as a gift or refuse to make it.
- If in doubt about any purchase, resist the temptation.

Of course, everyone makes mistakes, and you are bound to continue to make a few in the future. Follow these guidelines, however, and they'll only ever be small ones that you can easily sort out.

Look on every mistake you've made as a step towards good money management

Day Sixteen

DEALING WITH DEBT

Today it's time to look at debt. Most people have debts of one kind or another. The essential thing is that you feel you can manage any debts you have and that they're worth having. If not, it's time to start getting rid of them and to think about the thrill of being debt-free – and, if you've ever worried yourself sick about debt, you'll appreciate that being debt-free genuinely *is* a thrill!

When you take on any debt, you must decide whether it's worth the price to you. A mortgage is a debt, and most people feel it's worth taking it on to have a home they will eventually own. Almost all debts, however, cost a lot in interest. Before you buy anything on a credit card or a repayment deal, work out the interest you will pay and the REAL cost of the item. A dress can end up costing twice as much as the price on the tag if you pay for it in monthly instalments on a credit card. A car can cost you half as much again than the cash price if you pay for it over three years of financing. Only you can decide whether it's worth this kind of cost to you. Remember, if in doubt, say no.

A debt action plan

Perhaps you already have debts that you're worried about. Here's what to do:

1   Look at the interest you are paying on each debt. If it's high, or if the monthly repayments for all of them add up to more than you can afford, ask your bank or building society to give you a loan that will allow you to repay all the debts. You can then pay off the loan, which should be at a more reasonable rate of interest, over a longer period and at lower monthly instalments.

2   If you really feel in crisis over debt, go to a debt-counselling agency for advice. There are plenty of them around, and their experts will help you to sort it out and deal with creditors.

3   Steer clear of loan agencies offering you instant loans – they usually entail very high interest charges.

4 Remember that being in debt doesn't make you a bad person. It simply means that you aren't managing your money well. Make the decision today that you will deal responsibly with your debts, then begin to manage your money well.

Debt is a drain on you and your money. The simple truth is that life is better without debts. They can cause anxiety, stress, sickness and premature ageing. Deciding to live without debt (apart from a mortgage, which is acceptable debt) is a decision for freedom and a burden-free financial life.

What's the downside of saying no to debt? It may mean going without something you'd like to have, saving up for what you want or making do with an old model. Is that really so hard? Only if you let it be.

Debt is a burden you can live without – leave it behind

Day Seventeen

ABOUT THAT RAINY DAY

Today I want you to think about savings. Do you save? Or do you think that it's something you'll get around to when you're richer/older/better organized? Well, here's a useful tip:

Nothing makes you feel richer than saving your money.

Almost everyone dreams about winning big or earning an immense sum of money. They fantasize about the wonderful feeling it would bring, about all the things they'd do with the money and about never having to worry again. For some people, the dream does come true. Even if you do win, earn or inherit a fortune, however, you won't feel rich for long if you spend it all. Hanging on to some of your money is the key to feeling rich. And that's a fabulous feeling.

Also, the fact is that only a handful of people achieve sudden riches. So, while it's fine to dream, do it at the same time as using the money that you do have in the best possible way.

Think you can't afford to save?

Think again about not being able to afford to save. You can begin with just a small amount, but do it regularly, every month. Make an automatic payment into a savings account. Once you've organized it, forget about it. Don't be tempted to raid your savings – let them mount up and, when you can, increase the amount you pay in. Every time you remember that you have money saved, you'll feel good about it and so feel good about yourself.

Don't rely on dreams alone. And don't kid yourself that you'll get round to saving when things are easier. Saving will help to make them easier because it turns your thinking around. If you can afford to save, you must be doing okay and managing your money well. The more you believe this is true, the more you'll continue to manage better and better.

Make the decision today to keep more of your money. Money is for spending, but it's for spending wisely, not rashly. What could you do without in order to put a little money into your savings? Do you really need that new pair of shoes/outfit/CD/meal out? Or would you rather keep your money? There is always a choice, and, if you usually choose to spend, it might be fun to make a different choice and see how it feels.

Don't be tempted, though, to oversave. Hanging on to money too tightly is never a good thing. If you never spend and try to hoard it all, you stop the flow of money in and out, and you may find less money coming to you. Always remember that life is about finding balance, and so is good money management.

Begin saving today and feel richer every day

Day Eighteen

ATTRACTING MORE

Prepare to feel excited. This day is all about how to attract more money into your life and how to feel rich and fill your life with plenty. The wonderful thing is that, once you tune into abundance on one level, say, money, you'll find it easy to attract abundance in other areas of your life, such as love, success and happiness.

First of all, there's nothing wrong with having plenty. In fact, there's everything right with it. Having plenty doesn't mean that you're greedy, selfish or depriving others. There is more than enough to go round, and everyone deserves to have plenty. The main thing stopping you from having plenty may well be your beliefs. If you believe that you don't deserve money, or that you must stay poor or that you will always let money slip through your fingers, this is precisely what will happen.

Decide today that you will choose to believe in abundance and to attract wealth of every kind into your life.

Attracting abundance into your life

1   Always focus on abundance beliefs, such as 'I deserve to have plenty', 'I attract money easily', 'I always have more than enough'. Repeat these positive phrases to yourself if you find yourself worrying about money.

2   Start to notice the riches that come into your life. Notice when other people are generous to you, when you find a coin in the street, when you get a lower bill than you expected or a small win or a rebate of some kind. All these things are abundance coming into your life. When you notice them and appreciate them, you will attract more of them, and greater amounts.

3   Be clear about what you want. Rather than saying: 'I want to be rich,' decide what exactly it is that you want right now. For instance, you may want enough money to buy a car, or put down a deposit on a house or apartment.

4 Be generous. The meaner you are, the less you will find good things coming into your life. Generosity always attracts more to you. But don't give simply in order to get. Learn to give lovingly, without expecting anything in return. Give to charity, give little gifts to family and friends, give time and energy. This doesn't mean spending recklessly, but give what you can and never let fear of poverty stop you giving.

5 Think lucky. Imagine you are the luckiest person you know. Imagine everyone you know saying to you: 'How on earth do you do it, you just seem to get lucky all the time?' Walk around with a big smile on your face, feeling lucky. It won't take long for it to come true.

6 Cultivate an attitude of gratitude. That is, be thankful for all that you already have – your job if you have one, your possessions, the holidays and treats that come your way, the things you are given. Be grateful for your talents and abilities, your family and your home. Every night, instead of asking for more or thinking about what you don't have, give thanks for what you do have.

Follow this today and every day for the rest of your life. Make it part of who you are. Become known for being generous, relaxed with money and a lucky person. Expect to attract abundance into your life and you will.

In order to attract more, you need to believe that more is coming

Day Nineteen

BE YOUR OWN BEST ADVISER

I want you to make the decision today that you are your own best money adviser and that you won't allow anyone to make you feel stupid when it comes to money. There are plenty of people around, including professionals such as accountants, bank managers and financial advisers, who are keen to put you down and make you feel ignorant in an effort to sell you their products. Some of them do this in a very friendly way, so that it's easy to be taken in.

Of course, there are times when we all need to consult experts, and there are experts who will treat you like an intelligent person and give you wise advice. And that's the point. It's up to you to know the difference and to choose whom you consult about money matters.

A guide to using the experts

- Never, ever hand over all the decision-making about your finances to someone else, whoever they are.
- Trust your instincts. If something doesn't feel right, don't go ahead with it.
- Check everything out. If you're told that a particular product is the best, check it out yourself. Do some research to find out whether that's really true.
- Never make an instant decision, particularly if you're being urged to do so. Always think about it for a day or more, and consider the alternatives.
- Make absolutely sure that you understand what you're being offered or advised to do, and what the long-term consequences may be.
- Don't be afraid to ask experts to explain something in simple, clear terms. If they can't or won't, they're either no good at their job or trying to sell you something you should avoid.
- Bear in mind that only you know what you want and what will suit you best. That's why you are your own best adviser. No one else has your interests at heart in the same way.

Understanding financial matters does not have to be complicated or mysterious. If you want to open a savings account and you're not sure which is the best kind for you, shop around and compare interest rates and the terms and conditions. For instance, an account with a good interest rate may not allow you instant access to your money. Think about what you need and what will suit you.

Refuse to be a dunce. Never say things such as 'I'm no good with figures' or 'I just can't understand financial things.' Always tell yourself: 'I am great with figures, I can understand anything I need to.' Train yourself by taking leaflets and information home and reading them carefully, without pressure. Remember that you can take the time you need to understand what you want to understand.

Decide today to be wise and clever with money and to trust yourself

Day Twenty

STAY INDEPENDENT

Today I want you to assess how independent you are when it comes to money. To be financially successful and to manage your money well, it's important to be independent. That is, you need to make your own decisions, to take charge of your own money and to generate your own income, unless there is a particular reason why you can't.

Many otherwise competent adults remain childlike in relation to money, depending on others or reluctant to take charge of their own finances. Are you among them? If so, it will hold you back and limit your options. Depending on others is the same as giving them power over you and putting yourself in a weak position. If you're doing this, today is the day to reclaim your power and shout it from the rooftops.

Here are some of the ways in which people commonly keep themselves from being financially independent:

- Relying on hand-outs from parents.
- Accepting an unearned income from a partner, or anyone else, when there is no good reason why they shouldn't earn their own income (obviously the situation is different if they're bringing up children, studying, ill or caring for a relative).
- Borrowing from friends or family.
- Relying on someone else to make financial decisions for them.
- Having no bank or building society account and relying on someone else to process cheques.
- Blaming someone else for their financial problems.

If you recognize any of these, or if there are other ways in which you keep yourself from being financially independent, it's time to make changes. Financial independence is great for your self-esteem, it's exciting and it's enabling – you'll have far more freedom of choice when you stop relying on others.

Whatever excuses you're using to stay dependent on others, be willing to give them up. Many adults still rely on their parents, believing that this is okay because their parents hand over money willingly. But once you're an adult, you shouldn't

need money from your parents (or anyone else who's bailing you out). Stand on your own two feet, and feel good about yourself.

Here's what to do to be truly financially independent:

- Earn your own income. Give up excuses such as 'I can't find the right job', I hate working' or 'I just want to do one more training/study course.'
- Never borrow money without a clear, written agreement stating when you'll pay it back – and always stick to it. It's better to borrow from a bank than a friend, as this means it is clearly a business agreement.
- Open your own bank account and manage it yourself.
- Make your own financial decisions. Of course, it's fine to ask advice from people you trust, but make sure that the ultimate decision is yours.
- Stop blaming others. Take responsibility for the outcome of your financial decisions, even the mistakes.

Financial independence is precious and worth having. Decide today what you need to do to be truly independent. Thank anyone who's been helping you, then let go of the life rafts, take the plunge and swim on your own!

Be financially independent and welcome success into your life

Day Twenty-One

MAKE GOOD CHOICES

Now that you're making your own financial choices, it's crucial to make sure that they're good ones. You need to know that you are wise and clever enough to make choices that will bring you stability, security, prosperity and peace of mind. You don't need to be trained as an expert or to have unique skills to make such choices. All you need are simple guidelines and confidence in yourself.

Guidelines for making wise choices

1   Find money mentors. By this, I mean people whose judgement and skill with money you admire. They needn't be experts. You may well have a friend who is good with money and who always seems well organized and competent financially. Ask him or her to teach you what they know.

2   Acquire the skills you need. If you think it would be useful to learn how to use your computer's accounting software, or to improve your maths ability, go ahead and find a relevant course which would suit you.

3   Always apply the simplicity rule: when looking at any financial choice, assess whether it's simple enough for the average person to understand clearly. If it isn't, don't go for it. Cons and bad deals are often wrapped up in complex jargon so that people won't spot them.

4   Decide whether something is right for you. We're all individuals with different needs and different life plans. That's why only you can know whether a financial decision is right for you. The way you organize your spending must be built around the lifestyle you want.

5   Calculate whether you can afford it. This is really the key question. Never be tempted to overstretch financially. Nothing's more miserable than struggling to keep up with payments and demands. Always allow a margin, or comfort zone, and plan on things costing more than you expect.

6 Never rush any financial decision. Take time to think about whether it's right for you. So many mistakes are made through haste and shysters and salespeople know this all too well. People selling anything from timeshares to washing machines will try to draw you in on the spot, insisting that the deal is only available right now. Never fall for this one – a good deal doesn't need to be rushed.

One of the key elements of making good decisions is knowing that there is always a choice and that the position you are in now is the result of choices you've already made. If they haven't been so great, decide today to turn things around and begin making good choices. You'll find that things improve very fast once you do.

Never make a choice in order to please other people. If they don't like the choice you've made, then that's okay. If they're disappointed or angry, remember that this will pass and it's not your responsibility. Your responsibility is to do the right thing for you, while respecting and not hurting others. If you give in under pressure, it will damage your self-esteem and your relationship with the other person.

Take your time and make the right choices for you

Day Twenty-Two

MONEY FOR FUN

Today feel free to remember that money is not just for serious things; it's for having fun with as well. Being too frugal, duty-bound and solemn about money will only make you miserable – not to mention everyone around you. No matter how tight things are, it's still important to put a little money aside just for fun and play.

Money is not meant to make you feel guilty, miserable or burdened. It is there to make your life good, and, the more wisely you spend it, the more you'll enjoy life. Having fun is part of wise spending. After all, what's the point of working hard, planning well and organizing your money if you forget to enjoy the fruits of your labour?

What is fun to you?

Take a pen and piece of paper, and write down ten things you really enjoy. They might include riding a rollercoaster, visiting a comedy club, skiing or swimming, dancing the night away at a party, enjoying a midnight picnic or going on a shopping spree. Or you might love indulging in a day of beauty treatments, getting together with friends in a café or spending a day on the beach.

Of course, not all ways of having fun involve spending money. But some do. Once you know how you want to have fun, you can build it into your spending plan. If you're part of a couple, you might decide to plan for things you can do together, such as a special meal out, a weekend away or a trip to the theatre.

There's another aspect to fun and money, and that's to learn to take troubles more lightly and to use your fun side as a resource. The most important time to have fun is often when you feel least like doing it – when things are difficult, when there seem to be problems all around you, when you feel broke. Sometimes the breakthrough comes when you can approach your problems in a humorous and light-hearted way. Or it comes after you have let yourself forget your problems and simply enjoyed yourself. You can then see things in a whole new light.

Remember that nothing is so awful that you can't laugh about it. Try saying your problem out loud, then add 'Ha, ha!' at the end. For instance, 'I've no idea how to pay off my debts. Ha, ha!' It may sound crazy, but your problems will seem less awful and less daunting, I promise. Being able to bring a light touch to a serious situation is a great skill to have. Laughter can help untangle knotty situations when nothing else can. I'm not suggesting that you be irresponsible. Only that you use the power of humour, fun and lightness to help you solve problems.

People who know how to have fun are special. Although we seem to possess this ability naturally as children, most of us lose it as adults. If you find that you tend to be too serious and never have fun, take a fresh look at your life. You may decide it's time to make some changes.

Do something fun today. Laugh, play and enjoy yourself. Let yourself be happy, and let money help you have fun.

You deserve to have fun and enjoy yourself with your money

Day Twenty-Three

GOING WILD

Today I want you to look at those times when you decide to go wild, to splash out and to say: 'To hell with it, I'm going to spend no matter what.' Almost everyone has moments like these. Christmas is a prime example. For many people, despite promising themselves to cut back or to be careful, a sudden rush of spending fever overwhelms them and they shoot way over budget or stick things on credit cards, caught up in a wave of excitement and promising themselves to deal with it later.

Bank managers know this syndrome well. So do all financial advisers. Christmas is the most tempting time of all, as mass spending is going on. If everyone else is doing it, why not you, too? It's a bit like mass hysteria – very, very catching.

Why not join in? Here's why not:

- Picking up the pieces after overspending is demoralizing and exhausting.
- After the wave of excitement comes the wave of worry – it lasts a LOT longer.
- Two months after Christmas, almost everyone will have forgotten what you gave them. In one recent survey, not a single schoolchild asked could remember, eight weeks on, what their parents had given them for Christmas.
- The items which seemed so essential, so exciting and so worthwhile at Christmas will often be gathering dust in a cupboard a few months later.
- If you pay for something with a credit card, then pay off that amount in monthly instalments, the final cost of the item will be three to four times the originally price. With this in mind, look at potential purchases and quadruple their price before you buy. Are they still so exciting?

If you want to go wild at Christmas, plan it! Work out, roughly, what you think you spent last Christmas. That's how much you need to save before this Christmas. The best way is to divide the amount by 12 and set that sum aside each month. When Christmas comes, you just spend what you've saved. Forget credit cards.

Other 'go wild' times such as birthdays are just the same. By all means enjoy them, celebrate and be generous. But don't spend for the sake of it, and don't spend money you don't have. You can always choose to make presents instead;

there are loads of things that anyone can make very cheaply. Or set a limit for each present and look on it as a challenge to find something lovely for under that limit.

The truth is that going wild just isn't worth it if it takes you into financial hell. The grovelling to bank managers, scrimping and scraping afterwards cancel out the brief thrill of the overspend.

Count the cost of going wild before you do it

Day Twenty-Four

COMFORT SPENDING

Most of us comfort spend from time to time, and that's fine. Some people do it so much, however, that it tips them into financial hardship, and this is when the problems really start to multiply. Instead of bringing comfort, their spending simply causes more misery, which in turn often leads to more comfort spending, creating a vicious circle.

Comfort spending is what you're doing when you spend money to make yourself feel better. The idea is to take the focus off unhappy feelings, whether they be loneliness, anxiety, depression, a broken heart, grief or any other painful feeling. Spending money on something you like gives you a temporary buzz, a lift, which masks the unhappy feelings. But the buzz is brief, and it's often followed by a low. So you need to spend again to get the buzz back.

This is what is happening with shopaholics. Usually women, shopaholics spend and spend, getting into debt and amassing cupboards full of things they often don't ever use or even unwrap. The point about this kind of comfort spending, just like any addictive behaviour, is that it doesn't work. In the long run, it won't help at all with the unhappy feelings – in fact, it only intensifies them.

Do you have any comfort-spending habits? Do you reach for a credit card when you feel low? Buy another pair of shoes? Spend money you don't really have or could use more wisely on something else? If you do, it's time to stop. This is not as hard as you might think. Once you understand why you comfort spend, you can choose to change the pattern.

Guidelines for controlling comfort spending

1   Don't be afraid of painful feelings, whatever they are. Try saying to yourself: 'They're only feelings. If I'm miserable, that's okay, there's nothing terrible about it and nothing I have to do to fix myself.' Painful feelings fade much sooner if they're acknowledged and not suppressed.

2   If you want to comfort spend, set yourself a spending limit which won't damage your bank account. Take that amount with you in cash and don't spend any more. Cut up your credit cards if you are often tempted to use them for a quick fix.

3 Give yourself some real comfort. Comfort means feeling safe, warm, comfortable and cosy. Try curling up with a soft blanket, a beautiful scented candle and a good book. Find out what really gives you comfort, then do it when you feel down. Perhaps it's a walk in the woods, a chat with a friend or a cuddle from someone who loves you.

Make the decision today to stop damaging comfort spending and to give yourself real comfort when you need it. Comfort means being kind to yourself, not creating problems for yourself.

Swap comfort spending for true comfort and feel the difference

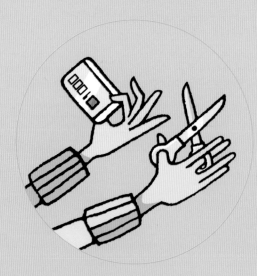

Day Twenty-Five

GIVE IT AWAY

Today I'm going to encourage you to give your money away. Yes, I do mean it!
Few things in life are more satisfying, uplifting and rewarding than being generous
to others. It has the added bonus of drawing money to you and increasing your
abundance as well.

When money is tight, people are in debt or they're having trouble managing
financially, they tend to go one of two ways. Either they're overgenerous, giving
away money and presents which they simply can't afford to buy, or they become
mean, hanging onto every penny and only grudgingly buying gifts when they have
to. Does either of these patterns sound familiar? To which group do you belong?

If you're overgenerous, it may be what got you into financial difficulties in the first place. Being overgenerous is the result of wanting approval and to be liked – which means your self-esteem is low. Being mean stems from poverty-consciousness, fearing there isn't enough to go round and that you have to hang onto what you've got. In both cases, people confuse money with love. Overgenerous people think they can buy love. Mean people think they won't be loved, so they must hang on to the crumbs they have and look after themselves.

If your behaviour with money follows either of these patterns, take today to stop and think about what you're doing and decide to change the pattern. Swap what you're doing for true generosity. Cultivate this in yourself – you will feel better about yourself, better about life and better about money.

True generosity means giving:

- Because you really want to, just for the sheer joy of it.
- Without expecting anything in return.
- What you can afford.
- With love, from your heart.
- When the time feels right, not because the calendar says you must.

Bear in mind, too, that the other side of giving is receiving. In order to give generously, you must be able to receive and accept generosity from others. Most people find it is far easier to give than to receive. Do you put obstacles in the way of receiving from others? Are you grumpy and ungrateful, or embarrassed by or feel uncomfortable with acts of generosity towards you? If so, you can begin to turn these feelings around. Being unwilling to receive means you feel you don't deserve good things and acts of love. Tell yourself today: 'I deserve all the love and generosity which comes my way. I will receive it with joy.'

Don't forget that both giving and receiving begin with you. Give yourself small gifts and acts of kindness. Receive them willingly and with pleasure. By both giving and accepting abundance, good fortune and acts of kindness with an open heart, you will attract more of them into your life.

To give and to receive are both acts of love

Day Twenty-Six

LOOK AFTER THE SMALL CHANGE

It's time to ponder the little things in life. Why? Because it's the things you spend small amounts on which you justify to yourself most easily and which all too soon add up to large amounts indeed.

Think about the time you take to make a decision about a really big purchase, such as a house, a car or even a holiday. You want to know exactly what's involved and whether it's a good investment. With small outlays, it's often very different. You fancy that miracle new face cream, gorgeous bracelet or cute handbag, and snap it up without thinking for more than a nanosecond or two. You probably justify it to yourself, telling yourself that you can afford it, you'll live cheaply next week, do without something else. The truth is, however, that for most of us this happens over and over again. And these 'small' things become big!

Lucy was a teacher living in a large city and sharing an apartment with a girl with whom she wasn't getting on. She was fed up because she never seemed to have any money and couldn't afford a place of her own. On top of that, her old car was about to fall to pieces, and she couldn't afford a new one.

After a month of life coaching, Lucy had turned her life around. She took a long, hard look at her finances and realized that she was spending a lot of money on extras she didn't really need. Top of the list she compiled were shoes. She would

buy a new pair every week and had cupboards full of them. Lucy made the decision to stop throwing her money away and start saving. Six months on, she had bought a car in good condition and put a deposit on an apartment of her own.

Analyse your spending to see how many 'small' things you purchase and where you could save. What have you got six of that you don't even use? Could you take lunch to work instead of buying it? Could you buy cosmetics more cheaply? Borrow a dress instead of buying one? Give a friend a gift you made yourself instead of buying one? Walk to work sometimes instead of taking the train or bus? Give up convenience foods?

The point here is not that you have to live like a pauper or do anything you hate doing. It's that when you take a long, hard look at your spending, there is often so much money which goes on little things you barely notice and which end up simply taking up space or being thrown away half-used. Once you realize this, you can choose where to cut back and keep your money, and where you want to spend it.

Do it today!

Exercise

Write down your last three impulse buys, then think about how important they are to you now. The thing you just 'had to have' has probably already lost its allure, hasn't it?

Now identify three areas where you can cut back your spending, without causing yourself any hardship. Write down the amount you will save daily, and see how much you will have saved after a month. That's money you still have and can choose to save or to spend on something else.

When you think carefully about smaller buys and choose to skip some of them, you suddenly find that you have more money than you thought possible. It's liberating!

**Feel instantly richer by choosing
to say no to the non-essentials**

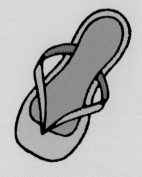

Day Twenty-Seven

MONEY AND MOODS

It's time to reflect on the link between money and moods. We all have moods – they're simply a part of life. And moods change, like the weather. When your mood is good, your spirits are high and things feel easy. When your mood is bad, your spirits are low and worry and anxiety can easily set in.

Your mood can have a significant impact on the way you handle money. When you are feeling low, everything seems harder, other people seem better off, making or managing money feels like hard work and success looks a million miles away. In a low mood, problems seem overwhelming. In a great mood, the very same problem can appear small, manageable and unimportant.

Think about a recent worry you've had. Perhaps you were anxious about a bill, an overdraft or a fall in income. You probably focused on it a lot, turning it over in your mind many times. Now imagine you have just had the most amazing piece of good fortune. Perhaps you met the man of your dreams and fell in love. The feeling of being happily in love is wonderful; the world glows with sunshine and joy. In this light, your problem looks small. You know you can handle it. You make a decision about what to do easily, without fretting.

This is the effect that moods can and do have. It's important to recognize when your mood is clouding your judgement and when you should put off financial decisions. Never try to solve problems or waste time worrying about them when you feel low. You'll just make yourself feel more depressed and solve nothing. Self-pity is like treacle: you get stuck in it and, the more you struggle, the deeper you go.

The next time you feel a bit blue, make a decision to put off all worry and anxiety about money. Tell yourself: 'I'll deal with that later.' Wait for the mood to pass. You can speed this up, if you want to, by talking to yourself in positive ways and being kind to yourself. When you're feeling good again, you can give some time to sorting out your finances and making decisions.

Remember, too, that problems, like wounds, often heal themselves if left alone. Picking away at a scab makes it worse. So does worrying about a problem over and over again. Leaving it alone and trusting that all will be resolved often leads to a solution, sometimes without you having to do a thing.

Be patient with a low mood – it will pass, often much sooner than you expect. Be glad of a good mood and enjoy it. And always be aware of the effect your mood is having on the way you handle your life and your money.

**Make money decisions when your mood is good
and make things easy for yourself**

Day Twenty-Eight

TRUST

Today I want you to look at the issue of trust in relation to your money. Do you trust yourself to handle money well? Do you trust others with whom you have to share financial matters? Do you trust that you will always have enough and need not worry? For most people, the answer is yes in some areas and no in others. For some, there is no trust anywhere. Yet trust is vital if you are to feel relaxed and successful when it comes to money.

What or who don't you trust around your money? To trust is to have faith that the outcome will be for the best or that people will do what they say they will. Trusting yourself is the same. It means having faith in yourself to cope and to do what you set out to do. It's about believing that all will be as it should be.

If you have doubts, ask questions. What are your doubts about? Have you been let down in the past, by yourself or someone else? If so, trust must be rebuilt. The way to do this is to be trustworthy yourself and to choose to deal with people who have proved themselves trustworthy.

Begin with your instincts. Trust yourself to know who will treat you and your money fairly. Stop dealing with anyone who won't. Look at the behaviour of others. Is it straightforward, honest and reliable? Above all else, look at your behaviour in relation to money. Has it been less than trustworthy in the past? Have you promised yourself to do something but not done it? If so, you can begin to turn this tendency around. There are bound to be other areas in your life in which you have been totally trustworthy. Knowing this will show you that you are capable of being trustworthy. Now believe that you can handle money in the same way.

Learn to trust yourself
Make three agreements with yourself today. Put them in writing and stick to them. They might include agreeing to:

- Pay your bills within three days of receiving them.
- Update your accounts once a month.
- Pay back any money you owe within a certain time.

- Stop spending on certain items.
- Keep within your budget.
- Buy yourself a small treat once a week.
- Sort out your tax/pension/will.
- Save a small amount every month.

Keep to these agreements you have made with yourself, and you will soon begin to trust yourself. An agreement with yourself may not seem important – after all, you can break it, and no one else will know that you have broken it. But it's actually more important than any other kind of agreement. Keeping an agreement you have made with yourself gives you a sense of being authentic, honest, trustworthy and worthwhile. It boosts your self-esteem and will give you more of a buzz than any spending spree can.

**Keep trust with yourself and know
that you are worth a million**

Day Twenty-Nine

SET YOUR AIMS

Dedicate today to working out your aims for the future and deciding what your goals will be in your financial life now that you have examined it more closely. So far you've done a great deal to get your finances in order and to take charge of your money and manage it well. By now, you will be feeling more confident, more in control and more optimistic about money than you ever have before. This means it is the perfect time to look ahead and decide where you want to go from here. Doing this will give you goals to work towards, keep you on track and reinforce the new habits you have learnt. It's all too easy to let things slip and find yourself back in a mess again. Choose not to do this, and decide instead to keep money matters simple and effective.

Exercise

Take a pen and piece of paper, and write down the money goals you have for the future. Here are some of the things you might want to include:

- Being completely debt-free.
- Managing your money without needing credit cards.
- Saving regularly and building up a really significant amount.
- Owning your own home outright.
- Earning money doing a job that you love.
- Reviewing your finances once a month.
- Keeping up your record of spending.
- Always feeling that you have plenty of money.
- Being more choosy about how you spend your money.
- Learning all you need to know about financial matters relevant to you so that you can continue to be your best adviser.

Add any other financial goals you'd like to achieve. Now divide your list into long-term aims (such as owning your own home, changing your job) and short-term ones (keeping up your spending record, becoming better informed). Think about what's going to be involved in keeping on track and reaching your goals. Do you need to open an extra savings account to build up a deposit to buy an apartment or house? Do you need to start looking for a job that you enjoy more and which also pays

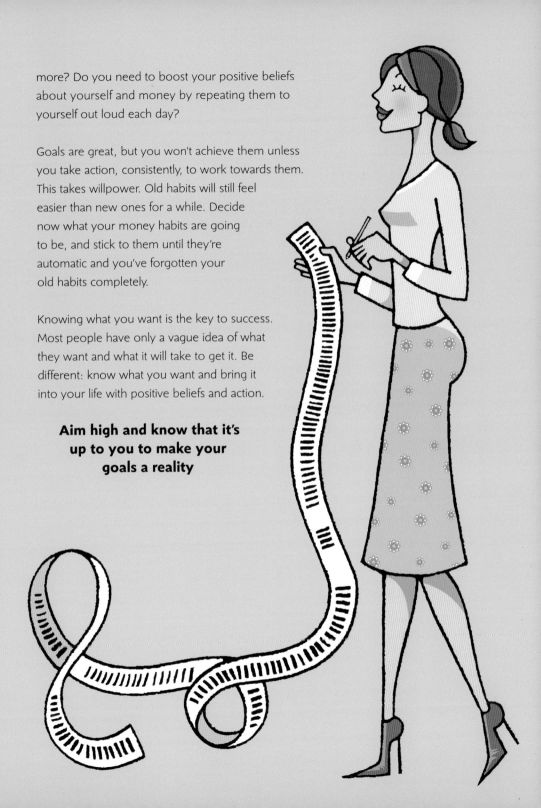

more? Do you need to boost your positive beliefs about yourself and money by repeating them to yourself out loud each day?

Goals are great, but you won't achieve them unless you take action, consistently, to work towards them. This takes willpower. Old habits will still feel easier than new ones for a while. Decide now what your money habits are going to be, and stick to them until they're automatic and you've forgotten your old habits completely.

Knowing what you want is the key to success. Most people have only a vague idea of what they want and what it will take to get it. Be different: know what you want and bring it into your life with positive beliefs and action.

Aim high and know that it's up to you to make your goals a reality

Day Thirty

CELEBRATE!

Well done! You made it through to the end. If you have carried out the challenges set for you each day, you will have given your finances, and your attitude to money, a complete overhaul. I hope that by now you're not afraid to handle money, you're aware of just how talented you are with money and of the great potential for success that you have, and you trust yourself to be your own wisest financial adviser.

I hope, too, that you now know how to attract abundance into your life. I trust that more and more is coming your way every day and that you're enjoying every minute of it. I know that you will be making wise choices and that often your choice will be not to spend, but to keep your money and enjoy the sense of security and plenty – not to mention self-control – that this brings.

Here are the things I want you to celebrate about you and your money:

- You can attract what you need, and what you want, into your life.
- You have power over your money and won't hand control to anyone else.
- You can afford to be generous and can enjoy receiving, too.
- You know who to trust and who not to trust with your money.
- You will never allow any 'expert' to make you feel small or ignorant.
- You truly value what you have.
- You know how to comfort yourself without spending money.
- You are independent and make wise choices when it comes your money.
- You know the secrets of good, simple money management.
- You know how to have fun with money.

So much to celebrate! If you have these skills now, you can carry them with you for the rest of your life and never be afraid around money again. Remind yourself that, even if disaster hit and you lost your job or all your possessions tomorrow, you would cope. You would pick yourself up and carry on, as what you can never lose are the inner resources that lead to success.

Be proud of yourself, and enjoy your money. After all, that's what it's for!

**Celebrate the joy of being successful
with money – now and for ever**

A FINAL WORD

You're now firmly on the fast track to the financial success that you deserve. Nothing can stop you from being successful with money if you really want to be and believe that you can be.

We live in a world of plenty. Some people know this and enjoy their share. Others live in constant fear of not having enough and aren't able to relax and enjoy what they do have, or to draw more to them. Money is energy, and, as with all energy sources, there are universal laws which govern it. Energy needs to keep moving, not to remain static. This is why it's important to keep money flowing in and out smoothly, and to be generous. With money energy, like attracts like. Hence the more you have, the more you will attract. As with other energy sources, there is plenty of money in the world, enough for everyone. Poverty is the result of our misuse of this valuable resource.

You absolutely can choose to make money your ally, your support and a great source of pleasure. Just like having a fit and toned body, having a fit and toned financial set-up makes you feel great. You have all the resources you need to stay in charge of your money for ever and to create the financial life you both want and deserve. So go for it!

Resources

FURTHER READING

Carlson, Richard, **Don't Worry, Make Money**, London, Hodder & Stoughton, 1998

Dowling, Colette, **The Myth of the Money Tree: Women's Hidden Fear of Supporting Themselves**, London, HarperCollins, 1998

Orman, Suze, **The Courage to be Rich**, London, Vermilion, 2000

Roman, Sanaya, and Packer, Duane, **Creating Money**, Tiburon, CA, H J Kramer, 1988

Temsi, Carolyn, and Handley, Caro, **Money Wisdom**, London, Hodder Mobius, 2001